Sunrise

(Collection of poems)

Abiathar Zadok

First Published 2008 by

StyleCom ventures

National Library of Nigeria C-I-P Data

Zadok, Prince Abiathar

Sunrise

PR 9387.6.Z17S958   AACR2   821

ISBN   978-978-48459-0-8

Cover picture: Abiathar Zadok

DEDICATION

To the blessed memory of my beloved sister, late Mrs. Bitha Caver Bute (Nee Zadok) whose joy it was to see me write and hear me read.

ACKNOWLEDGEMENT

At the dawn of my romance with poetry, I took my first squiggle to the table of my literature teacher. Her bright encouraging smile after going through "On the Grave" my very first poem, was the tonic that spurred me on. Thank you, Mrs. Zarma for that encouraging smile.

I am grateful to my parents for teaching me to appreciate the simple things of life.

My editors Mr.Ken Ike and Dr. Emman Usman Shehu. My friends Dr. Seyi Adigun and Lady Gesiri Bresibi-Dorgu are appreciated for their critique and useful suggestions.

I apologise for my any short coming in this work and my inability to mention all the people that contributed to this project in one way or the other.

May I conclude by thanking Gift E. Orji for typesetting and most importantly, Victoria and Veno; my wife and daughter, for their support and understanding during the sorting and compilation of these pieces.

CONTENTS

AUTHOR'S NOTES

Through the squinting eyes of a toddler I beheld the beauty of sunrise. The permanent picture cast in gold, travels with me through the stages of my voyage. I have like most travellers (at one point or the other) grappled with gloom and thick dark nights. Times and again nights have disappeared, storms calmed and dreams blossomed to realities.

Toddlers, teens and adults from different pedestals have divers experience of sunrise and understandably so. These are the collections of a life starting out in poetry, written at sunrise, presented to the world at noonday. (The pieces have retained their original form despite the passage of time).

Remember, whatever stage you are in your voyage, there will always be a sunrise.

Abiathar Zadok

CALLING THE SPIRITS

I summon you, spirits
Come!
High winds and waves
Move the stubborn mountains.
Talk!
The sweet yester jingles
Must resound where you reign

I summon you, spirits
Come!
Repossess the remains
Awaken!
Yes, reinvigorate the once envious life
Threatened by
Encroachments

I summon you, spirits
Come!
Rekindle the pride
Of our fathers
In our priceless heritage.

RATTLE SNAKE

Like the flooding of the sea
Wash ashore the waters wealth
Our moral values float away.
Like erosion eats the earth
Rust drain our vital roots
Green moments
Not lost in time
A people great
And envied too
Woke up to find the wild grasses grow
Where our fathers planted trust.

When the strayed strangers came
Who point their noses to the skies
The crooks who stole bequeathed wealth
And the pride of fatherland
Like the tale of Devil's child
Who chopped his mother's breast at birth
So they came
We housed and clad

Sunrise

We showed them men could love and trust
Alas, they do not understand,
'Cause they know not what it means.
We protected them from themselves,
While they learnt our arts and trade.

But who tames a rattlesnake?
Our fathers knew,
But they thought,
They could also learn our love.
Lo! Before the sun could rise
They broke our band
And took our gold.

Like the flooding of the sea,
Like erosion eats the earth,
So the flood washes the wealth
Of our waters
By and by.

THE WOMAN I WILL MARRY

I will marry the daughter
Of my stepfather
He took my mother
From my father
At gunpoint.

He will see it done!
I will marry
His beloved daughter.
The turpitude
Held in heritage,
She shall transfuse
To be welcomed
By my brothers.

Spineless she shall be
Warming the floors of my domain
Till together we rebuild
The broken walls of
My father's house.

When the vain pride is gone
And decency takes its place
I'll wipe away the memories
Of yesterday's cruelty.
Then
His daughter,
My sister,
My wife,
My beloved one,
Shall abide.

Abiathar Zadok

PETITION OF A PICCANINNY

A bus I boarded
Had a boy;
A handsome boy
In ugly frame.
Scrawny,
Peckish and peevish,
He looked.
I sat by him
And raced my lips:
You look so pale
So beaten and out
Can I in anyway
Touch your soul?

No!
Thank you,
I do doubt much

I've rambled long
In morbid ropes
And nurse no hope
To see sunrise.
My Pa,
They said,
Has gone to rest;
A wealthy
Nice and Goodman too.

My life he left to mum in trust,
With all that brings
A decent life.
But decorum wondered
Far from her,
And left her
Drain to dust in mind.
Like mad
She took a man and left,
Not caring if I live or die.

The engine soon came
To a stop.
Our conversation
Ended too.
Tears paint my eyes
Blood red.
When the wind of memory blows
The petition of the piccaninny
To mind.

THE BLIND

Son: Heartless men pass by our street;
            Short-sighted,
            Pumped up in pride.
            A greedy mutant
            Here we have.

Father: A bird must spread its wings to fly,
            But when it dives
            In honey pot,
            Flight becomes a wishful dream;
            Its wings are clipped
            Its strength will fail,
            It must be pitied
            Little child.
            He's neither mad nor blind
            You see?
            He both resides
            And rule this place.
            A warrior great
            He stood to be;
            Humble,
            Humane,
            And a rock.

Abiathar Zadok

He sought to serve
The common man,
We handed him
The common purse,
In no long time
A malady struck;
His eyelids
Rolled down in folds,
Photophobia
Fobbed his sight,
The true daylight
He does not see,
His wisdom ends
Within the walls
Of his belly
And his purse.
His mum and dad
In anguish lives
For many sons
Play the blind.

ONLY FOOLS

Here he comes;
So rouge and rude,
Beaming bright in ugliness.
Arrogance and pride
Propel his steps.
Dressed in rags
Devoid of grace;
Dirty
Bitter
Hot and
Rash.
Robbed of honour,
Robbed of worth,
Dejected
Desolate
And despised.

Once he reigned
The present junk
Now a toy for lunatics
Out of favour
Out of date
The hills
The valleys
Despise him,
He has no place in the Inn.

Beaming bright in ugliness
He pinches
Prickles
And pierces too
So he is swept
Far out of gates
And toyed with only by the fools
Oh Truth!
Now,
Toy for fools.

SURVIVAL TRAP

From the afar came a guest
He begged into a hunter's hut
Learning the hunter's trade
The hunter's custom soon he led.

Times and seasons soon pass by
Days and years were so gone by
The guest in the huntsman trade
Scored himself the highest grade

The hunter took it for jest
Without regard he plied his trade
Next, he heard command rolled out
Only hunt the way I say or don't

Abiathar Zadok

By and by the guest had grown
From a guest to a co-landlord
All who saw him thought a clown
And the clown tighten his hold

With time, he seized the hunter's bow
On the strength of equal right
So they called it final blow
The brawl lasted day and night

I SING TO THE SIMPLE

When a groomed guitarist
Strums the strings
An ocean of sweetness flow
When the plumy voice
Of a gifted vocalist
Rules the stage
Melody and rhythm vibrates.

To the birds
I play my drum
Slung on ancient wings
The music streams
From the roots
Of the spring
A common beat.

Tunes from time
I sing to the simple.

Chapter 2

LIFE

TIMES

I saw him
Who once was feared
Sitting outside
On the line
Looking up
Like seed of grain
For rain.

LIFE

Mountains and valleys
Slops and plains
Crisscrossing
The landscape wide
Eagles flying
In the sky
Ants go speeding
On the ground
To and fro
The voyage goes

Fashions fade
And some will soon
Stars are twinkling
Just the same
The more men plough
The more confused
Who knows the weight
Of the missing chain?

Lot of birds
Have walked the sky
Epochs pass
And ages come
Constant is
The darkest night
Circling on the roundabout

TURBULENT WAVES

Oh! Sea of turbulent waves,
How many have ridden the route?
Dear exhilarant package
Of antique confusions,
We present ourselves.

The boat afloat is ours,
In the track of travellers gone.
Ours is the smallest boat;
To others the biggest on sea.
Our hands cup our heritage
Caged in the caves of our dreams.

We possess the inability to tell;
Illusions from perceptions,
Reality from contraptions.

Sunrise

We set sail,
We know not how,
Till time dictates,
And we alight.

In the course of our ambivalence
Oh!
Mighty mystery;
Sea of turbulent waves.

THE ORIGIN

A seed,
Sprouted from the Source.
Like the cedar
Spread out hands;
Numerous
Diverse
Plump and pale.

Multi-shades
Human seeds
Dressed in races
Long in trace;
sprouts of a seed
Branches and spread.

The shadows down the trees
You see,
Dark and light spots
On the ground.
Leaves and gaps,
Caused them all.
As weather,
Climate,
Place,
And time.
Leaves and gaps,
Caused them all.

Whenever the sun shall set,
That same moment shadows cease.
Beneath the tree
Shall be no spots.
Man seedling,
Was never two.

ANTITHESES

Once I greatly wondered why,
Sun and stars
Keep running round.
And there it was
Right in my nose,
Breathing daily
In and out.

I have also wondered why,
Birth and blood
Are always one.
And there it was
From birth of time
Life and death
Has since been so.

Have you ever wondered once
What is it that holds the sky
From slipping down into the sea?

Perhaps you must have wondered why
Smiles and sadness change places
Like dry and rainy seasons do.

Don't you ever this forget,
There is a front to every back;
To every night, a breaking day.

SAVINGS

If the holy never withers
And there be no change in the weather
If only the tree which blossom today
Shall not shrivel tomorrow

If change shall cease
Where there be no yesterday
But man is lame
To the hands of the clock

If the sun shall never set;
And a bright day turn to night
Just as nights
Turn to days

If time is frozen
Dreams dancing the streets
Where youth forever glow;
I would walk thinking of no difference.

THE ON LOOKER

I have a brother
Right at home
A football fan
Of great repute
He never stepped
On football pitch
But plays better
Than players all.

When he sits
To watch the game
His mouth and legs
Do watch with him
He heads
And kicks
And dribbles in dreams
He has never touched
A ball
But plays better than players
All.

SEASONS VERSE

Let the season sing a verse
Listen well to the roaring rain
Hear the rattling of the sea
And the prattling of the birds
Dawn and dusk in ceaseless chase
Dry season slitters
The rains rumble
Harmattan brings its gusty fangs
Sweet sweat
And sour soup
Pleasant juice and faulty fruits
The world spinning
On its wheels
The sky has not
A constant style
The clouds are still
On endless march.

A TREE I SAW

Under the tree I once sat,
I stand.
Flowers bloomed,
And leaves evergreen.
Sweet and gentle breeze
Was here.

In a dream,
The simoom blew,
The leaves were gone,
The comfort too.

Flood from nowhere
Broke the banks,
Foresight stood still in blindfolds,
Wonders went wild
Beyond a word.

Man must learn,
The dance steps of change.

NEW YEAR EVE

Through the heart of forest far
To the belly of valleys vast
Burning dreams
Shadows and substance
From the ash
And beats of old drums
Play the pulse
Of a twelve month trip,
Standing at the door
Of a brand bright dawn.

The dying tree
Is red in roots
Detached leaves
Yellowing
Browning fast
The drops are dried
In the throng.

The wind is back
From journeys great
Its bags are filled and full to brim
Above
The moon in gentle steps
Makes the circle full and done
Soon it slumps to spring anew
A phoenix full of larger hopes.

THE SUNRISE

I never cared to know
But once there I was
Sitting on the stone
In front of father's hut;
Head upwards
Eyes wide open
Like a watch man
On a watch tower.

It was morning
And the Sun in his shell
On the stone in front of father's hut
I sat.
Since the first crow
To see the sunrise.
Sun in his shell,
Awaken from his sleep
By the crow of the morning cock.

For long I've waited
So long have I been sitting
I know it will rise
But when?
I do not know.

Still sitting
On the stone in front of father's hut
I could hear the pigs squeak.
In my tired waiting,
There blew the sunbeam siren
In majestic procession
Dawdling slowly
So lazily.

Then
Came the colours of the sun;
Dazzling white and golden
Blazing pink
On the edges,
Enclosed in a gloriole,
As I goggled through my goggles.

Sunrise

I have seen the sun pop out
I knew it would
To grow our plants
And strengthen us
Yet
Slowly it rises
So slowly.

Chapter 3

RELATIONSHIPS

MERRY BELLS

They are ringing merry-bells
Up the sky and
Down the ground
Here it comes
The gentle drops
Yeah
I feel its tender touch
Ringing merry bells in me
I hear the rolling of the drums
Rip-rip and rat-ta-ta
Tah-ra-ra
Ra-ra-ra
Dropping on the roof
And me.

I LOVE ROSES

In the mid of a June
At the strike of a mission
In the midst of business
An angel descended

Full of light
A glaring flower
Of resplendent roots
And sucrose stems

In the midst of my wonder
In the state of my confusion
A rosebud
God's best creation

Sunrise

A crystal jewel
Sparkling clean
A charming chocolate
A glorious treasure

Transfixed!
I was lost,
Only found in love with a Rose
For which roses bloom
In the mid of June

Abiathar Zadok

STRONGER THAN IRON BARS

Rolling chameleon style,
The mighty crawling snail-like,
Like a captive held in chains,
Bound in fetters of disquiet,
Stronger than iron bars.

In the strength of many rocks
Came the mighty lightening flash
And the clangs of thunder sound
I'll have to go
Or else I'll die:
The raining
Is tearing my housetop.

MEMORIES

Glorious times
Of childhood days
We walked happy
In dirty rags
Sucking milk
From mummy's breast
Getting all we need for free.

When we sick
She steams and stiff
And faint in mind
Like water waves
Nothing else pleases her
Like pellucid eyes
And glaring teeth

Those were the days
We ruled the kings
And rode on mummy's back like ' horse
And when we like
We make mum mad
By crossing legs and crying loud.

MOTHER

Dearest desert honey spring
Your juicy flow
Has never dried
Your credit line
Has never failed
To pay the price
Of endless love
Tireless
And relentless flow.

Through the childhood tube
You stood;
My fence
My source
My safe harbour.

Store of kindness
Mountain like
Your stream of patience
Wide and deep
Your constant love
A ceaseless gift
My first and ever
Brightest star
My ocean
Of unrivalled flow.

LUST

Woaa-woooo!
Blows the wind
Curtsy force
The trees
To bow.

Leaves
Hooked,
In a wingless flight;
Dangling
Dancing on branches.

Some are scattered
On the ground,
The mighty wind
Is blown
And gone.

AGAINST THE TIDE

Who shall cross path
With my ways
To soar above the stars
And rays

Who shall look beyond the sun
Beyond the golden
Morning flex
To the darkness of its roots

Who shall fly above the wind
Into the clouds
Above the stars
Who can stand against the tide?

Sunrise

If you must cross path
With my ways
Look beyond the shining sun
To the darkness of its roots.

HERE I COME

Distinctively
Here I come
My spikes let loose on the track
The marathon ended a dash
And runners took their hits
In turns
We nudged each other on
With smiles
Bunch of happy birds
In flight.

Distinctively
On the tract
Beneath the tree
Where time stood still
The birds were gone
And smiles were weaned

The leaves were no more
Where they were.

This new season
Stands men bare
And reality rills
The blindfolds off.

COMFORT

You did not look back
When we called
When the noose was on the neck
We looked up to see the stars
Black
Were they twinkled bright.

Where were you
When hell was here
We did not know the day would dawn
'Cause we saw the death of hope
Who knew that life could new begin
When the sun descended here
With its hot and piercing eyes
And the covering clouds were gone
Then in sorrow's jaws we laid

You did not look back
When we called
When you were we needed most
You left us dancing jazz in jail
Now you rap knocks on our door?
Go Comfort!
We need you not.

NO FRIEND NO FOE

Friends and foes
Are changing frames
Your friend a foe
To someone's friend

Friends and foes
Perspectives sold
The borderline is;
Who
And when.

FOES FOR FRIENDS

By his name he was the rock
And he does not look a reed
Free I felt to rest my back
That's when I went crashing my head

It was in March the wind was grey
And the cold held at bay
We met on the way
To be one with the wind

Our destination seemed the same
At least the steps suggested so
The vacation I thought shared a name
I did not see his tool; a knife.

MAN

Some are bound
From birth to be bad
And these lots abound
How sad

Since the chase
Of sun and stars
At the birth of river bars
Man has made
The mountains mad.

HYPOCRITES

It's not your faces
That we hate
It's not your colour
Frame or height.

We did not hide
From you our fears
Thought the logs have blocked
Your ears.

Not for us, for you we fear
Least your deeds, their fruits eat you
Human-looking whimsical monsters
Look like just and pious preachers.

PREGNANT BROOK

Behold the exploded
Pregnant brook
To set record
And beat the book,

Not only break
Out of tune
When the show of shame was peak
But picked on oceans as it rolled.

This day shall man dispute
His sight
Against the truth
Made plain by light.

HAIL MARY

Condemned I stand
Needing no judgment
I ask no clemency
For my cruelty
Seeking no pity
Deserving non
So dreadful I am
Jehovah hates me
The devils favourite

In vain
You waste your precious time
In the protocol of justice
My case need not be mentioned
Charges needless reading
To all allegations
Heard and unheard
I plea guilty

I have committed the unforgivable sin
My five fingers
I opened in His direction
I spat on God's face
For long
The unforgivable sin committed

Hail Mary
Mother of God
Will you pray for me a sinner?
Like my papist pals
Lacking a recidivist
With me in parity
But cannot pray for themselves
Be my proxy
Solicit
Intercede
And plead my cause

I possess not the courage
Of the prodigal son
To seek my father's
Unmerited favour
Be my advocate
Mother Mary
Pray for me.

Hey! Mary
Do I really need your prayer?
Have you done it for others before?
Can you really do it for me?
No Mary
I need not
Your prayer

I will crave the indulgence
Of the Most High
His prerogative of mercy
To grant
For guilty
I stand
Awaiting the fulfilment
Of the cause of justice

And if in parley
I
Not a party
Mary
Oh! Mary
Do not
Pray for me.

GONE ARE THE DAYS I ADORE YOU

Too late!
Pray, plead no more
No amount of it
Can call back the blowing wind.

My mind is made
My resolve resolute
My soul sticks to one thing
My eyes are glued.

Empty wind
And daylight dreams
Saps the source of my soul.

I have heard you say;
'Forgive, forget
I have seen my sin
My blood transfused.'

Too late my dear
Credulity gone
No force
Terrestrial
Fat or flat
Can patch up this broken egg.

Too late, I say
Too late my dear;
Gone are the days
I adore you.

THE DIFFERENCE

I have not come here to lead
You can take back your blade
Not to strive
Just to survive

I shall not take your
Father's throne
So I threaten not your
Crown.

CHOICE

I will rather be wrong
But right in me
Than be right
And wrong in me
Among the two
I have a choice.

Chapter 4

MIXED GRILL

HAPPY BIRTHDAY

While roses
Bloom and scent
And silver twinkle in the stars
Outwit both
In scent and shine

While you trek
This travelling path
Be home
To all that makes life thick
May marvels
Cap your everyday
And smiles
Take you to bed
Each night.

GET WELL SOON

I heard the joke
Is now on you,
The saddening news
Elated me.
Sounds of smiles
Echoes loud.
A rooted rock
Is my faith
I know you will
Blow it off
With a jab.
So relax, my friend
Relax,
Sleep in smiles
And have your rest

Abiathar Zadok

No sick bed
Can pin you down
Take a break
And bounce back soon.

SHADOWS IN A DREAM

I saw you coming through the door
A million and ten thousand times
In your gallant silky ropes
Elegant steps and juicy smiles
All but shadows in a dream.

There you stand
Dressed in your jokes
Mingled truth
And little lies
Wherein I wallow
Now and then

I saw you
As you said I would,
Yesterday at last
Was here.
Also shadows in a dream.

Abiathar Zadok

I saw you coming through the door
A million and ten thousand times
Acting up
And cooked old tales
Dear friend;
Shadows in a dream.

C.V

I cannot turn
The streams round?
Yeah!
I cannot make the Beatle buzz
I am no Harvard
Economics groomed
I am no business Admin Don
My tree of experience
Is slim
The know-how
True
It seems
I lack.
We also know
I lack the lack.

DOKIN BABA

Dokin Baba;
Is daddy's horse.
Brown and shining in the sun.
Quiet,
But a masters breed.
Always limping, looking frail.
While hunting,
Or out racing,
Dokin Baba,
Beats the best

LIBERTY

Time and time and time again
The battle rages on and on
Since when the whistle blew
In the garden made his choice
Man was bound
A slave to self
Liberty does not exist
Not where I've seen
Green grasses grow.

DEPRESSION

The wind ceased
The day is dark
The world stands still
And you,
Miss in the legend?

The night is come
Darkness covers the earth
The stars go blind
And you,
In the darkest mist.

The lambenting sky
Pose prosaic
Drabness being deciphered
And you,
Crestfallen.

Sunrise

I have seen the end;
You said to yourself,
Having hobbled hell alive
In my confabulation with depression.

EXPLOSION

Rioting tempest
Crushing beast
Gruesome monster
Murderous master.

Brutal silence
Thunderous furnace
Vicious vipers
Venomous strikes.

Could men cage
Or calm the storms?

Balls of brimstone
Ocean of flames
Erupt!
Display your impotence
Volcanoes of human weakness.

Chapter 5

DATH
AND
DEPARTURE

CELL MATE

You sit smiling on your swivel chair
Your cigar rings go round in the air
Your other hand the whisky cup
And the ash keeps piling up.

How come you wear the familiar look
I see on the palm wine taper's face?
When smile became a burden to take
And misery made to wear a dress

Your difference speaks out loud and clear
The diverse backgrounds stand to bear.
Yet one the unity of the soul,
To fate are you bound one and all.

I KNEW YOU

I knew you once,
When rocks ran in your marrow.
When everything was certain, including tomorrow.
Now everything I ever knew, I doubt twice.

What became of yesterday?
Those strong tissues, solid as stones.
Are these peeled cassava or bones?
 Where is the reality in today?

This cruel truth leaves one on ice:
Knowing you don't have a say
On the way, you have to lay
Not a little of a choice.

ON THE GRAVE

I gave birth
To me
Yesterday;
On the grave
When he died.
Whom alive
I never knew.
When the mourning birds
Converged,
Indifferent,
I watched their flight.
On every tree
They mourn the dead,
In the midwife's arms
I laid.
First, I learned to feel the world
There I also learned to cry.

GOING

I have seen them
Going
Gone
Friends fly
Relations roll
And others ooze
Thousands queuing
Thousands quitting
 Some in sordid
Wordless ways
Others pleasantly in sleep
I mourn for you
After our smiles
Barely
Two seconds ago.

I have seen them
Going
Gone
In legions as rivers flow
Both the feeble
And the strong
Others groaning
Others laughing
All that creeps
And all that breathes
Different shapes
But single doom

I have seen
The foetus float
The four-leg kid
 The two and three.

Sunrise

I have seen
My age mates melt
Younger ones
And older ones
Loved ones
Lovers on the line
I have seen
The grasses burn
Trees wither
And birds gone blue
I have seen the widows wail
The orphans ouch
And sadness smile.

I have seen
The balloon bust
The bomb blast
And the bracket close
Adventures go out of hand
Accidents that must occur
Onward still the list may go.

I have seen them
Going
Gone
How
When
Where
And why
Ask the seer
Who would tell?
I have seen
And I have seen
How sudden the balloon bust
Without warning
Without a knock
All that creeps
And all that breathes
Different shapes
But single doom

TILL THEN

In the event of my peregrination
If in the event of my jungle roaming
The bomb of my race strikes
Find me on the mountains
Running with the rocks

Till sunset
The tussle shall be
You Wilkins hold your waters
The wild wind chase
Is done.

THE JUST DIVIDER

Visitors of no appointment
Withdrawers of no deposit
Swaggering at will
Since the primeval
Did somebody dare ask why?

Abel the progenitor
Your offspring are non-disciplined
Having neither respect nor regard
For the young and the old
The rich and the poor
Male and female alike

Yet nurtured
In a way worth my praise
None deluded by all invented principles
Masters of no time pass by
Their steps unknown
Yet very sure

Pilots of the plane of no discrimination
The levellers of hills and valleys
Like thieves they arrive
Without invitations
No knocks on doors
Leaving behind,
Their seals and scars.

GOOD BYE

Oh! My wiggly butterfly
Wish I do we never part
Here I pose
Without a choice
Like a fish held in a hook
I cannot stay
The line is drawn
The sinker is up
I'll have to go
Hard times they be
We cannot help
When we just must say;
Good-bye!

ABOUT THE AUTHOR

Sunrise is the collection of the first adventure of Prince Abiathar Zadok in poetry. The poems in this collection are largely presented as written in mid 1980s.

Prince Abiathar Zadok. Lives and work in Abuja, Nigeria.

www.ingramcontent.com/pod-product-compliance
Lightning Source LLC
Chambersburg PA
CBHW070539030426
42337CB00016B/2274